The real story of

Flight 19

The unsolved disappearance of six US Navy aircraft in December 1945

Real story of...

Book 1

D1711087

Contents

About '*The Real Story of...*' series of books 4

Introduction...6

Prologue 10

Chapter 1: NAS Ft. Lauderdale 13

Chapter 2: Navigation Problem Number 1 20

Chapter 3: 5th December, 1945 25

Chapter 4: I don't know how to get to Fort Lauderdale 30

Chapter 5: If we could just fly west we would get home! 39

Chapter 6: Everything looks wrong!....................................52

Chapter 7: Into the Bermuda Triangle 57

Chapter 8: Meanwhile, back in the real world... 64

Chapter 9: Lt. Charles Taylor 72

Chapter 10: The Real Story of Flight 19..............................83

Conclusion 100

Bibliography 103

About the Author 106

Other '*Real Story of...*' books...107

About 'The Real Story of...' series of books

You may be wondering what makes 'The Real Story of...' books different to the vast number of other books on mysteries? The answer is really pretty simple: This series takes some of the best-known mysteries of the twentieth century and subjects them to detailed, rational, unbiased analysis and follows wherever the evidence leads.

I believe that makes these books different to the majority of books which begin with a particular point of view and then selectively interpret the evidence to support that theory. The kind of books which build a whole wobbly edifice of conjecture on top of a foundation of half-truth and misinterpretation. I don't find that kind of book particularly satisfying and, if you're reading this, perhaps you don't either?

I'm not a skeptic or a debunker by inclination. That is to say, I'm not going to write-off a potential solution just because it seems unlikely or because I don't have direct, personal experience of it. However, if I'm to accept, for example, a solution that involves the paranormal, I'm going to want evidence to back that up. My own background is in engineering (I also have experience as a pilot) so I tend to look for pragmatic, understandable cause and effect in any given situation. I don't start by assuming that aliens, ghosts or reptilians must be the answer to any particular question. But then I also once spent six months sharing my home with a poltergeist, so I don't start by assuming that solutions that go beyond the bounds of accepted scientific knowledge are impossible either.

I go back to source to check evidence wherever possible and I provide a bibliography to allow you to do the same. I am constantly surprised at how other books and websites accept evidence without checking its veracity. Once a particular *'fact'* is repeated often enough, it becomes accepted as true whether it has any basis in reality or not and that can skew any attempt at providing a solution to a mystery.

I can't promise a complete solution to every mystery in this series, but I do promise not to bullshit. If I quote a fact, you can be assured that it has been checked and then double checked. If I propose a solution, it's built on these facts and not on some fantasy that I'm trying to peddle. This world of ours is strange enough that we really don't need to make this stuff up.

So, are you ready to take a detailed look at some of the strangest and most inexplicable mysteries of the last hundred years?

Introduction

To most Americans, the world in December 1945 was a stable and predictable place. World War Two was over, the good guys had been victorious and the Nazis and the Japanese had been completely vanquished. America possessed the most powerful military forces in the world and it was also the only country to understand the secret of the most terrifying new weapon of the twentieth century: the atomic bomb.

However, what no-one realized at the time was that the world was on the cusp of enormous change. The next major international conflict, the Korean War, was less than five years away. By the time that war began, the Soviet Union would have its own nuclear weapons and the world would be coming to understand the full horror of the notion of *'mutually assured destruction.'*

Instead of producing another triumph of arms for the free world, the war in Korea would end in a bloody stalemate which saw the country split into a democratic south and a Communist north. This was to be followed by another costly, futile and ultimately unsuccessful war in Vietnam. In 1945, America looked unbeatable, its scientists were the foremost in the world and the country had every reason for unbounded optimism. Twenty-five years later, things would look very different indeed.

Even for the young men training to become naval aviators at the US Naval Air Station at Ft. Lauderdale in Florida in 1945, it was obvious that major changes were coming. The aircraft on which they were training were propeller driven relics of the past. The future clearly belonged to the new-fangled jets which were just beginning to come into service with the US Navy and the US Army Air Force.

The very nature of combat flying was also changing with the first guided weapons just a few years away. Flight 19 used torpedo bombers which had proved to be decisive weapons in World War Two. However, torpedo bombers would not play a major role in any future conflict and they were soon replaced by aircraft capable of firing guided missiles from tens or even hundreds of miles from their target.

The future would not turn out to be quite as rosy as it looked in America in December 1945. But, the fourteen men who took part in Flight 19, a routine training flight, would not see that future. All would be dead long before it arrived. They took off and flew their aircraft into fair weather on a flight over the ocean to the east of Florida. It should have been a simple training flight but none of the men of Flight 19 were ever seen again and the thirteen-man crew of a flying boat sent out to search for them also disappeared. No trace of any of the missing aircraft or men has been found since.

This was one of the worst peacetime losses of life for US Navy aviation. Even more baffling, there was no obvious reason for the loss of life. To lose an aircraft is, unfortunately, not especially uncommon: naval aviation is and always has been a dangerous occupation. But to lose six aircraft in a single incident with no obvious cause was very uncommon indeed.

The US Navy investigated and proposed a solution. However, for many people the scenario put forward by Navy investigators was unsatisfactory in one important way: it suggested what might have happened, but it provided absolutely no clue as to why it might have happened.

Interest in the fate of Flight 19 might have died away had it not been for two completely unrelated incidents which took place over the next couple of years. On June 24th 1947 Kenneth Arnold, a private pilot, sighted a group of very odd looking aircraft while flying in Washington State. Subsequent media reporting called these *'flying saucers'* and suddenly, the idea of alien visitors flying over the earth became widely discussed. Then, in January 1948, a US Air Force Pilot, Captain Charles Mantell, died when his aircraft crashed after being sent to intercept and identify an unidentified flying object over Godman Field in Kentucky.

There was a massive media response to these two events – it suddenly seemed that flying saucers in the skies over America were not only real, they might also be hostile. It didn't take long for people to remember the mysterious disappearance of Flight 19 and to wonder whether flying saucers might not also have been involved in that incident too? This notion gradually gripped the popular imagination and, when Steven Spielberg was looking for a striking and dramatic first scene for his 1977 movie about encounters with aliens, *Close Encounters of the Third Kind*, he chose to show the discovery of the aircraft of Flight 19 in the Sonoran desert in Arizona.

Over the years, the melding of fact with fiction has led to Flight 19 being associated with UFOs and aliens, or with strange environmental occurrences such as giant waterspouts or even with the Bermuda Triangle. I believe that, if we go back to the original evidence, it is possible to demonstrate that the real story of Flight 19 is simpler, but no less mysterious.

Prologue

Florida is a good place to learn to fly. The weather is generally warm and predictable and there are no high mountains to make navigation dangerous. At the beginning of World War Two, Florida was also fairly sparsely populated and that's why the US Navy established a number of Air Stations in the state at locations including Banana River, Daytona Beach, Jacksonville, Key West, Miami and Richmond. One of the largest Naval Air Stations (NAS) in Florida was NAS Fort Lauderdale, situated around twenty miles north of Miami. NAS Ft. Lauderdale was originally intended as a satellite field for NAS Miami, but by 1945 it had become one of the largest fields operated by Naval Air Operational Training Command and specialized in the training of pilots and aircrew for the TBF/TBM Avenger torpedo bomber.

The Grumman TBF Avenger (Avengers manufactured by the Eastern Aircraft Division of General Motors were basically identical but were designated TBM by the US Navy) entered service in 1942 as a direct replacement for the obsolete Douglas TBD Devastator. The Avenger was principally intended as a torpedo bomber though it could also drop conventional bombs. The aircraft carried a crew of three: Pilot, radioman/bombardier and rear turret gunner.

Although it was a single engine design powered by a 1,900hp Wright Twin Cyclone radial engine, the Avenger was a large aircraft and the heaviest single-engine type ever operated by the US – the take-off weight of the Avenger was over 18,250 lbs compared to, for example, 12,000 lbs for late models of the P-51 Mustang fighter.

The original model of the Avenger, the TBF-1, saw combat in the battle of Midway in June 1942 and the aircraft was involved in almost every subsequent major naval action in the Pacific theatre. By 1945, the current model was the TBF-3 with a more powerful engine and wing hardpoints for mounting drop-tanks and rockets. However, by 1945 the US Navy was already looking to introduce jet fighters to naval aviation. The first jet took off from a US aircraft carrier in June 1946 and it wouldn't be long before propeller driven aircraft such as the Avenger were looking rather old-fashioned, though the TBF wouldn't be completely retired from active service until the early 1960s.

The war in Europe formally ended on 8th May 1945 and on 15th August 1945 Japanese forces surrendered following the dropping of atomic bombs on the cities of Nagasaki and Hiroshima. The training of new aircrew for the navy declined with the end of the war, but it did not cease completely – those who had started learning to fly during the war were allowed to complete their training. In 1944 the

US Navy trained over twenty-one thousand new pilots. In 1945, this had dropped to just over eight thousand.

This wasn't surprising. In December 1945 the world was at peace and the US Navy was not involved in conflict anywhere in the world. But, US foreign policy was also changing – the isolationism of the pre-war years was replaced by a new doctrine of 'containment.' This was based on a perceived need to limit the international spread of Communism and required the US to be able to undertake what became known as power projection, the ability to deploy armed forces rapidly and in various parts of the world. The US Navy, and in particular its aircraft carriers, formed an important part of this new policy and so, even with World War Two over, the training of naval pilots and aircrew continued in Florida albeit at a lower level than previously.

Chapter 1: NAS Ft. Lauderdale

Even during the most intense parts of World War Two when there was a constant need for new combat pilots, it wasn't easy to be selected as a trainee US Navy pilot. Candidates had to have completed at least two years of college, had to be unmarried, with perfect health and a very good standard of fitness.

Once selected, Naval Aviation Cadets had to pass four, ten week *quarters* in ground school before they were enrolled in Primary Flight Training. This took place at Naval Air Station (NAS) Pensacola in Florida where students learned the basics of flying in Naval Aircraft Factory N3N or Stearman N2S biplane primary trainers, generally known as *Yellow Perils* because they were painted all yellow and were often flown erratically by inexperienced trainee pilots. No matter how careful the initial selection process, this was where most trainees dropped out. Many students just weren't able to develop the flying skills required to meet the very high standards set by the navy and on average, 40% of cadets dropped out during Primary Training.

One of the 'Yellow Perils', a Naval Aircraft Factory N3N-3 Canary trainer in 1942.

Those who survived Primary Flight Training graduated to Basic Flight Training where they practiced instrument and night flying, formation flying and gunnery on the North American SNJ advanced trainer (the navy designation for the AT-6 Texan). Pilots were also given an introduction to carrier landings at this stage, though this was done on specially marked sections of runway rather than on an actual aircraft carrier.

The final stage of pilot training was Advanced Training where pilots would receive instruction on the types of aircraft they would fly in combat. For those selected to fly the Avenger, Advanced Training took place at NAS Ft. Lauderdale in Florida. On completion of this stage of training, pilots would then be posted to operational units.

Training at NAS Ft. Lauderdale included bombing as well as the use of torpedoes – the Avenger could carry either a single Mark 13 torpedo, one 2,000 pound bomb or up to four, 500 pound bombs in its large bomb bay. With the ability to fly out to a maximum range of 1,000 miles, the Avenger was also capable of mounting missions at longer range than any previous US Navy aircraft, and this meant that training in accurate navigation was also critical.

In most World War Two aircraft, navigation was done by using a compass plus visual indicators where possible – the pilot used the compass for basic navigation and simply looked for landmarks such as rivers, mountains and cities to confirm their position. However, for naval pilots who might be flying for long distances over water, this wasn't possible. Instead, these pilots used *'dead reckoning'* to estimate their position. This meant that, if they flew on a known course at a known speed for a known length of time, they should arrive at their destination.

But, this could be affected by head, tail or crosswinds. These were predicted by professional naval weather forecasters in advance of each flight. Unfortunately, winds are fickle things and these could often be different to the forecast, leading to aircraft ending up way off course. Ultimately, in those pre-GPS days the only way to be certain of an aircraft's position was for the pilot to be able to see and recognize a known landmark.

On aircraft such as the Avenger, there was one additional electronic aid to navigation – the Identification Friend or Foe (IFF) transponder. This was an electronic beacon that sent out a signal that could easily be picked up by friendly radar. During wartime, this was most often left switched off because it might also make the aircraft easier for an enemy radar units to pick up. However, if switched on, this could be seen by friendly radar at long range which could then give the aircraft information via radio on the direction in which to fly to return to base.

TBM Avenger

Photo: Robert Frola

Radio communication to and from the Avenger was via a massive vacuum-tube radio set located in the long cockpit behind the pilot and this equipment was used by the Radio Operator/Bombardier. This area of the cockpit was also used to house the search radar which could allow the Avenger to find a ship from up to forty miles range. At the rear of the cockpit, in an electrically operated turret housing a single .50 caliber machine gun, sat the third member of the crew, the gunner.

Pilots, gunners and radio operators/bombardiers underwent training separately. Pilots were officers, often Ensigns or 2nd Lieutenants while the other members of the Avenger crew were generally enlisted naval air-crewmen.

NAS Ft. Lauderdale was commissioned in October 1942 specifically to provide operational training on the Avenger aircraft. By the end of World War Two it had become a huge operation which included more than two hundred buildings and three main runways. The facility included a Base Administration division comprising twelve departments and an Operational Training Unit comprising eight departments. Between its opening and its closure exactly four years later in October 1946, NAS Ft. Lauderdale trained over 2,000 Avenger pilots from both the US Navy and the US Marine Corps in addition to pilots from the British Royal Air Force and the Canadian Air force.

NAS Ft. Lauderdale in 1945

Photo: Naval Air Station Fort Lauderdale Museum

https://www.nasflmuseum.com/

The Avenger was generally recognized as a pleasant and docile aircraft to fly but sadly, by the time that NAS Ft. Lauderdale ceased operations in October 1946, ninety-four aircrew had died in training accidents. This wasn't thought to be a particularly high proportion of trainees to lose - learning to fly complex and powerful military aircraft is inherently dangerous and during the war, almost one third of all US Navy aviation deaths were due to *non operational crashes* which included training and ferry flights. More US Navy and Marine Corps pilots died in training than in combat.

Photo: US Navy Museum of Naval Aviation

By December 1945, flying training at NAS Ft. Lauderdale was being scaled-down. Only cadets who had begun their training before the war ended were allowed to continue with their courses. In 1946 a completely new training program for the training of naval pilots was introduced, the Naval Aviation College Program (NACP), and the flying portions of this seven year course were mainly undertaken at NAS Corpus Christie in south Texas.

Chapter 2: Navigation Problem Number 1

The syllabus for trainee Avenger pilots at Ft. Lauderdale included several '*Navigation Problems*', exercises designed to teach cadets the rudiments of navigation while out of sight of land. Many of these exercises also included mock bombing or torpedo attacks.

In each case, a group of aircraft was sent out on the exercise together. Each group of aircraft was designated as a flight and given a number according to the order in which that particular group was scheduled to leave Ft. Lauderdale. So, the first group of aircraft scheduled to fly on any given day would be designated Flight 1 with subsequent flights being numbered according to their scheduled departure order.

One of the aircraft in each flight would be flown by an instructor pilot while in all the other aircraft the pilots and crewmen were trainees. Cadet pilots were each given the opportunity to take turns to lead the flight during the exercise with the instructor monitoring their performance. It wasn't uncommon for cadets to become hopelessly lost during the early stages of navigation training. For this reason it was important that the instructor was aware of the location of the flight at all times so that, if required, he could take control and lead the flight back on to the right course.

Each 'Navigation Problem' taught the cadets how to use dead reckoning. This involved flying a known course at a known speed for a known length of time to arrive at the desired location. Three of the many instruments in the Avenger cockpit were critical to this type of navigation:

Inside the cockpit of an Avenger

Photo: Rama

The **Air Speed Indicator** (ASI) gives the speed that the aircraft is moving through the air in knots (1 knot = 1 nautical mile per hour. 1 nautical mile = 1.15 miles). However, this airspeed can be quite different to the speed at which the aircraft is moving over the ground. For example, an aircraft may be showing an ASI reading of 100 knots, but if there is a fifteen knot headwind, the aircraft will only be covering the ground below at a speed of 85 knots. For navigation it's necessary to estimate ground speed by allowing for head, tail or cross winds.

At the centre of the instrument panel, the **Gyro Compass** shows the heading on which the aircraft is currently flying. The Avenger was also provided with a simple **Magnetic Compass** as back-up in case of failure of the Gyro Compass. But, the sea off the coast of Florida is one of the only two places on the planet (the other is the Devil's Sea off the east coast of Japan) where a compass needle actually points to true north. Everywhere else, a compass needle suffers from declination, i.e., it points to magnetic north which may be anything up to 16° from true north. Pilots used to flying in other locations could find the lack of declination confusing and those who didn't realize this could find themselves way off course. The two compasses fitted to the avenger were completely separate mechanical devices and so, if for example, the aircraft suffered from a complete electrical failure which disabled the Gyro Compass, the Magnetic Compass would still function.

Finally, the Avenger instrument panel also featured a very accurate and reliable twenty-four hour **Electric Clock**. Using these instruments, cadets were able to monitor their course, speed and the length of time they had been flying on a particular course.

Navigation Problem Number 1 required cadets to fly four separate legs over the ocean east of Florida in a triangular route which would bring them back over land to the north of NAS Ft. Lauderdale. The route included bombing practice at Hen and Chicken Shoals, a group of small, uninhabited islands located between the coast of Florida and the island of Grand Bahama. The total distance flown was to be a little over three hundred miles. At the normal cruising speed of the Avenger (135 knots/150 mph), the total flight time including practice bombing would be around two and a half hours.

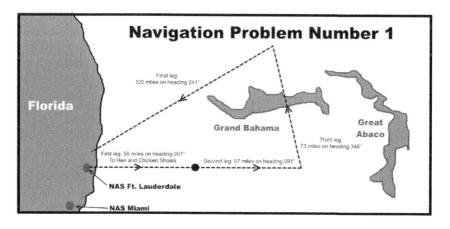

The **first leg** of the exercise required cadets to fly almost due east from NAS Ft. Lauderdale on a heading of 091° for fifty-six miles until they reached Hen and Chicken Shoals. There they would conduct a glide-bombing attack (using dummy bombs) on the wreck of the SS Sapona, a concrete-hulled ship wrecked there in 1926.

The **second leg** required continuing on a heading of 091° for a further sixty-seven miles to a small island, Great Stirrup Cay, at which point the flight would turn towards the north on a heading of 346°. During the **third leg** the flight would overfly the island of Grand Bahama and, after covering seventy-three miles and sighting Great Sale Cay, would turn back towards the east and the coast of Florida on the **fourth leg** which required a flight of one hundred and twenty miles on a heading of 241°. The fourth leg was planned to end when the flight crossed the coast of Florida somewhere north of NAS Ft. Lauderdale. At this point the flight would turn south and would follow the coast until they sighted their base.

This was a completely standard navigation exercise which had been flown many hundreds of times without incident by cadets operating Avenger aircraft from NAS Ft. Lauderdale.

Chapter 3: 5th December, 1945

The weather on the morning of 5th December 1945 was average for the time of year with a temperature of 67°F, gusting southwest winds, visibility of ten – twelve miles and the possibility of rain showers. The sea state was described as moderate to rough. A full day of flying training was expected but the weather was forecast to deteriorate towards evening with heavy cloud, rain and strong winds expected to arrive from the north.

Flight 19 on that day was a group of five Avenger aircraft. All were TBM models (Avengers manufactured by General Motors), four were older TBM-1C models and one was a later and more powerful TBM-3D. All had been re-painted in the new peacetime color scheme of overall dark blue. All were marked with the letters 'FT' ('F' indicating an aircraft based at NAS Ft. Lauderdale and 'T' indicating a torpedo bomber) with a unique two or three digit aircraft number. The letters FT followed by this aircraft number were also used as radio call signs.

Maintenance reports show that none of the aircraft had any known problems, all survival gear was present and all had full fuel tanks. However, each aircraft was missing one important piece of equipment – the cockpit clock. These accurate and reliable electric clocks had proved to be popular items with aircrew and maintenance workers and were often stolen. When the war ended, the navy stopped replacing these expensive items and the maintenance log indicates that none of the aircraft in Flight 19 had a cockpit clock – pilots were expected to use their wristwatches to monitor the time flown on each leg of the exercise.

The four aircraft of Flight 19 which were to be flown by trainee pilots were:

- **FT-36**, TBM Avenger TBM-1C, BuNo 46094. **Pilot**: Capt. Edward Joseph Powers Jr., USMC. **Gunner**: Sgt. Howell O. Thompson, USMCR. **Radioman**: Sgt. George R. Paonessa, USMCR.

- **FT-81**, TBM Avenger TBM-1C, BuNo 46325. **Pilot**: 2nd Lt. Forrest J. Gerber, USMCR. **Gunner**: None. **Radioman**: Pfc. William Lightfoot, USMCR.

- **FT-3**, TBM Avenger TBM-1C, BuNo 45714. **Pilot**: Ensign Joseph T. Bossi, USNR. **Gunner**: Herman A. Thelander, S1c, USNR. **Radioman**: Burt E. Baluk, S1c, USNR.

- **FT-117**, TBM Avenger TBM-1C, BuNo 73209.

Pilot: Captain George W. Stivers, USMC.

Gunner: Sgt. Robert F. Gallivan, USMCR.

Radioman: Pvt. Robert F. Gruebel, USMCR.

One of the aircraft, FT-81, would be flying the exercise without a rear turret gunner. A trainee gunner, Corporal Allan Kosnar, had originally been scheduled to fly in FT-81 in Flight 19 but he had asked to be excused the training flight as he had already acquired the required number of hours (and not, as some people have tried to suggest, because he had some premonition of impending disaster).

The only TBM-3D model in Flight 19, FT-28, BuNo 23307, was to be flown by the flight leader and instructor, Lt. Charles Carroll Taylor, USNR, an experienced pilot with over 2,500 hours of flying time who had piloted the Avenger in combat in the Pacific. Taylor had only recently transferred to NAS Ft. Lauderdale from NAS Miami and this was his first flight as an instructor and flight leader from his new base and the first time he had flown Navigation Problem Number 1. The crew in Taylor's aircraft was completed by the gunner, George F. Devlin, AOM3c, USNR and the radioman, Walter Reed Parpart, Jr. ARM3c, USNR.

Lieutenant Taylor was outranked by one of the trainee pilots, US Marine Corps Captain Edward Joseph Powers Jr., but Taylor was designated Flight Leader and had overall command of the flight. All the trainee pilots in Flight 19 were relatively experienced with around sixty hours of flying the Avenger and this was to be their third and last training flight before they graduated from NAS Ft. Lauderdale.

Flight 19 was scheduled to depart NAS Ft. Lauderdale at 13:45. The preceding flight, Flight 18, was scheduled to depart at 13:15 and was to fly the same exercise, Navigation Problem Number 1.

Five TBF Avengers in formation

Photo: National Archives and Records Administration

The trainees waited for their instructor in the briefing room close to one of the main runways, but Lieutenant Taylor was late. He didn't arrive at the airfield until 13:10 and, instead of going to meet with his students, he went instead to see the Aviation Duty Officer, Lt. Arthur Curtis. Taylor then arrived in the briefing room and explained the exercise to his students. The Training Duty Officer also attended the briefing and he noted that the aerologist's report produced that morning confirmed that the weather was expected to be *'favorable'* for the training flight. After the briefing, the students and their instructor went out to their aircraft and prepared for departure.

Due to Taylor's late arrival, Flight 19 didn't take off until 14:10, twenty-five minutes later than scheduled. However, this should have meant that they would arrive back at NAS Ft. Lauderdale before 17:00, well before sunset at 17:30 and before the forecast arrival of bad weather. All the aircraft carried enough fuel to keep them in the air for five – five and a half hours if required.

As observers on the ground watched, the aircraft formed up and flew off to the east in formation. No-one could have guessed that none of the aircraft or their crews would ever be seen again.

Chapter 4: I don't know how to get to Fort Lauderdale

Note: This chapter and those that follow contain transcripts of radio communications relating to the loss of Flight 19. These are taken from the official US Navy Board of Investigation report on the loss of Flight 19. This report includes testimony from witnesses, expert opinions and logs of radio transmissions. However, these logs of radio transmissions are not transcripts of recordings – radio communications were not routinely recorded in 1945. Instead, these are transcripts produced from either hand-written logs kept by radio operators or from the recollections of witnesses, so they may not be absolutely verbatim accounts of what was said.

Sometime between 14:30 and 15:00, NAS Ft. Lauderdale Operations logged two short radio transmissions which were assumed to have been made by aircraft in Flight 19. These were aircraft-to-aircraft transmissions which were only picked up by the operations center because the aircraft were still relatively close.

"I've got one more bomb."

"Go ahead and drop it".

This indicates that Flight 19 had reached Hen and Chicken Shoals and were carrying out glide-bombing practice there as scheduled (the flight from NAS Ft. Lauderdale to Hen and Chicken Shoals should have taken around twenty minutes).

A Marine Corps Avenger glide-bombing over Okinawa.

Photo: US National Park Service gallery

Another radio transmission between the aircraft of Flight 19 was overheard at around 15:40 and this was far from routine. In fact, it suggested that something was very wrong indeed. This transmission was heard by the senior flight instructor at NAS Ft. Lauderdale, **Lt. Robert Cox**, who was flying over the base in Avenger FT-74, waiting for a training flight to form up. Suddenly, he heard a broken and partially garbled radio message which suggested that a flight of aircraft was in trouble. He repeatedly heard a voice asking someone called Powers (presumably Captain Edward Joseph Powers Jr., the pilot of FT-36 in Flight 19) what his compass read. Finally, Powers was heard to reply:

> *"I don't know where we are. We must have got lost after that last turn."*

Lt. Cox continued to monitor the radio over the next fifteen minutes as garbled and broken radio messages between the aircraft of Flight 19 faded in and out. Cox overheard fragmentary radio messages that included: *"Does anyone have any suggestions?"* and *"I think we must be over the Keys."* By this time, Cox was sufficiently concerned that he abandoned his training flight and informed NAS Ft. Lauderdale Operations that he believed that a ship or a group of aircraft were lost and in difficulty. Ft. Lauderdale Operations (call sign NHA1) were not able to hear the transmissions from Flight 19 and relied on Cox to stay in the air over the base and relay information to them. After discussions with NHA1, Cox put out a blind transmission, hoping to reach the craft in distress.

> *"This is Fox Tare 74, will the plane or boat calling*

Powers please identify yourself so someone can help you."

After trying this several times, Cox finally heard a clear response.

"Roger, this is MT-28."

This transmission was almost certainly from Lt. Charles Taylor, the Flight Leader for Flight 19. However, he seemed to have become confused about his radio call-sign - he mistakenly initially identified himself as '*MT-28*' instead of using the correct radio call-sign of '*FT-28*'. "*MT*" was the identification used for torpedo bombers flying out of Miami, where Taylor had previously and recently been based. Cox replied:

"MT-28, this is FT-74, what is your trouble?"

Around 15:50 Taylor responded.

"Both my compasses are out and I am trying to find Fort Lauderdale, Florida. I am over land but it's broken. I am sure I'm in the Keys but I don't know how far down and I don't know how to get to Fort Lauderdale."

Taylor's response made no sense on a number of levels. Flight 19 was well over 100 miles north and east of the Florida Keys. Take a look at the map below to see where

Flight 19 most likely was at 15:50 – the circle shows a 65 mile radius round the turning point where the flight should have turned on to a heading of 346°. Depending on the direction in which they flew, they could have been anywhere within this circle but they certainly couldn't have been over one hundred miles away and over the Florida Keys as Taylor seemed to believe.

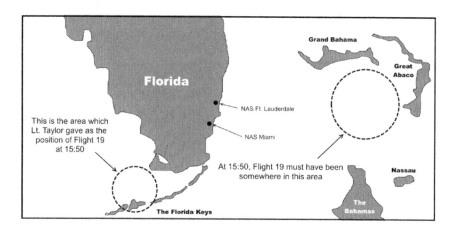

Taylor's comment that he didn't know how to get to Ft. Lauderdale also didn't make sense. Even if both his compasses had somehow failed simultaneously, all pilots in the area knew that if they were flying over the Florida Keys, all they had to do was place the afternoon sun off their left wing and they would be flying north, towards NAS Miami and Ft. Lauderdale. Realizing this Lt. Cox transmitted:

> "MT-28 this is FT-74. Put the sun on your port wing
> if you are in the Keys and fly up the coast until you

get to Miami. Fort Lauderdale is 20 miles further, your first port after Miami. The air station is directly on your left from the port."

Soon after this, Lt. Cox turned his aircraft south, towards the Florida Keys and transmitted again.

FT-74: "What is your present altitude? I will fly south and meet you."

FT-28: "I know where I am now. I'm at 2,300 feet. Don't come after me."

FT-74: "Roger MT-28, you're at 2,300. I'm coming to meet you anyhow."

FT-28: "We have just passed over a small island. We have no other land in sight."

It was clear by this point that Taylor and his flight were completely lost. The situation was serious but not yet critical. At this point the Avengers of Flight 19 had enough fuel remaining for another 3 - 3½ hours of flying, or perhaps a little more if they flew as economically as possible. Guessing that the lost aircraft were most probably Flight 19, Ft. Lauderdale Operations then contacted Lt. Cox with a question.

"FT-74, is the call sign of your contact MT-28 or FT-

28?"

Cox raised the question with Taylor.

> *"MT-28 this is FT-74. Please verify. Are you MT-28
> or FT-28? Over."*

At 16:26 Taylor responded.

> *FT-28: "Roger, that's FT-28, repeat FT-28. FT-74,
> Can you have Miami or someone turn on their
> radar gear and pick us up? We don't seem to be
> getting far. We were out on a navigation hop and
> on the second leg I thought they were going wrong,
> so I took over and was flying them back to the right
> position. But I'm sure, now that neither one of my
> compasses is working."*

> *FT-74: "You can't expect to get here in ten minutes.
> You have a 30- to 35-knot head or crosswind. Turn
> on your emergency IFF gear, or do you have it on?"*

> *FT-28: IFF gear was off, I am turning it on now. I
> am at angels 3-5."*

Cox transmitted to NHA1.

> FT-74: " *Flight of 5 planes leader is FT-28. He has
> his emergency IFF equipment on. Requests if he can
> be picked up on Fort Lauderdale radar gear."*

NHA1: *"Negative. He cannot be picked up on Fort Lauderdale radar gear. Tell FT-28 to have a pilot with a good compass take over lead."*

FT-74: *"FT-28, this is FT-74. Have a wingman with a good compass take over lead of flight. "*

FT-28: . . .unintelligible. . . *"radar. . ."*

This was good, if very obvious advice that Cox was offering. If Lt. Taylor really believed that neither of his compasses was working correctly, it would make sense to have one of the other aircraft in the flight do the navigation. Cox, who was still flying south towards aircraft he assumed were flying north up the Keys towards him became aware that the radio transmissions from FT-28 were getting weaker, which made no sense. In fact, it is almost certain that at this point Taylor, still hopelessly lost, was over one hundred miles distant and actually flying away from Cox.

FT-74: *"Your transmissions are fading. Something is wrong. What is your altitude?"*

FT-28: *"I'm at 4,500 feet."*

At this point, the battery on the ATC transmitter in Cox's aircraft went off-line and he was unable to make any further contact with Flight 19. Cox turned back to the north and returned to Ft. Lauderdale where he landed. He made no further contact with Flight 19. When Lt. Cox later gave testimony at the Board of Investigation into the loss of Flight 19, he was asked where he thought Taylor was during these radio communications? He told the Board:

> ". . . as his transmissions were fading, he must have been going away north as I headed south. I believe at the time of his first transmission, he was either over the Biminis or Bahamas. I was about 40 miles south of Fort Lauderdale and couldn't hear him any longer."

The Duty Flight Officer at Ft. Lauderdale on December 5th was asked the same question by the Board. He responded:

> "I... learned that the flight leader thought he was along the Florida Keys. I then learned that his first transmission revealing that he was lost had occurred around 1600. I knew by this that the leader could not possibly have gone on more than one leg of his navigation problem and still gotten back to the Keys by 1600."

In other words, it was clear to everyone except Lt. Taylor that Flight 19 could not possibly be over the Florida Keys.

Chapter 5: If we could just fly west we would get home!

Air-Sea Rescue Task Unit Four at Port Everglades (call sign NHA3) which had been monitoring communications between Lt. Cox and Flight 19 now took over communications with Flight 19.

> NHA3: *"Nan How Able Three to FT-28: . . . can you read us?"*
>
> FT-28: *"Affirmative. We have just passed over a small island. We have no other land in sight. Visibility is 10 to 12 miles. I am at angels 3-5. Have on Emergency IFF. Does anybody in the area have a radar screen that could pick us up?"*
>
> NHA3: *"Suggest you have another plane in your flight with a good compass take over the lead and guide you back to the mainland."*
>
> FT-28: *"Roger."*

At 16:31 the following transmission from Taylor was picked up by NHA3:

> FT-28: *""FT-28 to Nan How Able Three, one of the planes in the flight thinks if we went 270 degrees we could hit land."*

This was absolutely correct. All students at NAS Ft. Lauderdale were told that, if they became disorientated while flying over the Atlantic, they should simply fly a course of 270° (due west) or, if their navigation equipment failed, fly towards the afternoon sun. At 16:39 the Ft. Lauderdale Operations Officer contacted the Air-Sea Rescue Task Unit Four at Port Everglades by telephone to confer. It was agreed that a group of aircraft seemed to be lost somewhere over the Bahamas and that transmissions from the group were becoming more difficult to understand, suggesting that they were moving away from the coast. The Gulf Sea Frontier High Frequency Directional Finding Net was contacted to obtain a radio bearing on the flight's transmissions. Nothing more was heard from Flight 19 until 16:45:

> *"FT-28 to Nan How Able Three. We are heading 030 degrees for 45 minutes, then we will fly north to make sure we are not over the Gulf of Mexico."*

Clearly, Lt. Taylor had not heeded the suggestion that the flight head west. Instead, still believing that he was over one hundred miles to the east and over the Gulf of Mexico, he was leading the flight north east, almost directly away from land and safety, over the open ocean and into darkening skies and decreasing visibility. At around 16:50 NHA3 asked Taylor to switch his radio to the emergency frequency.

> NHA3: *"If you can change to Yellow Band (3000 kilocycles), please do so and give us a call."*
>
> FT-28: *"I receive you very weak. How is weather over Lauderdale?"*
>
> NHA3: *"Weather over Lauderdale clear. Over Key West CAVU. Over the Bahamas cloudy rather low ceiling, poor visibility."*
>
> FT-28: *"Nan How Able Three, Can you hear me?"*
>
> NHA3: *"Hear you strength three, modulation good. Can you shift to 3000 kcs? Over. FT-28, please change to 3000 kcs. . . .shift to 3000 kcs. Over."*
>
> FT-28: *"Nan How Able Three, How do you read?*
>
> NHA3: *"Very Weak. Change to 3000 kilocycles."*
>
> FT-28: *"Hello Nan How Able Three, this is FT-28. I can hear you very faintly. My transmission is getting weaker."*
>
> NHA3: *"Change to Yellow Band channel 1, 3000 kilocycles and give us a call."*
>
> FT-28: *"My transmission is getting weaker."*
>
> NHA3: *"Change to Yellow Band 3000 kilocycles and say words twice when answering."*
>
> NHA3: *"Nan How Able Three to FT-28, Did you receive my last transmission? Change to channel 1 3000 kilocycles."*

FT-28: *"Repeat once again."*

NHA3: *"Change to Channel 1, 3000 kilocycles."*

FT-28: *"I cannot change frequency. I must keep my planes intact."*

Photo: National Archives and Records Administration

Presumably Taylor was finding it difficult to maintain formation as the light began to fade and the weather worsened. He wanted to maintain radio communication with the rest of the aircraft in Flight 19 at all times, hence his unwillingness to change to the search and rescue frequency. However, because he was still heading away from land it was becoming difficult for shore stations to receive transmissions from Taylor and evidently equally

42

difficult for Taylor to receive transmissions from shore. At 16:56 Taylor failed to respond to a request from NHA3 to turn on his ZBX receiver, part of the TBMs direction finding equipment. After 17:03 several disjointed and fragmentary transmissions were heard from Taylor to the other aircraft in Flight 19:

> *"All planes in this flight join up in close formation."*

> *"How long have we gone now?"*

> *"FT-28 to all planes in flight, change course to 090°*
> *for 10 minutes."*

> *" . . .You didn't get far enough east. How long have*
> *we been going east?"*

During this period transmissions were also heard from angry and confused pilots in the other Flight 19 aircraft:

> *"Dammit, if we could just fly west we would get*
> *home"*

> *"Hold it: head west, dammit!"*

Although these pilots were not formally identified in the Board of Investigation report, it was believed that they were Capt. Powers (pilot of aircraft FT-36) and Ensign Joseph T. Bossi (pilot of aircraft FT-3). Whoever they were, the unidentified pilots were correct and Taylor was completely wrong. There presumably followed some heated discussion between the aircraft of Flight 19 though none of this was picked up by listening shore stations. At 17:16 another transmission was picked up from Taylor to NHA3.

> FT-28: *"Hello Nan How Able three, this is FT-28. Do you read? Over."*
> NHA3: *"Roger. This is Nan How Able Three. Go ahead."*
> FT-28: *"I receive you very weak. We are now flying 270° "*
> NHA3: *"Roger."*
>
> FT-28: *"We will fly 270 degrees until we hit the beach or run out of gas."*

Finally, Flight 19 was heading west, towards the coast and safety. At this point the aircraft had more than two hours of fuel left, sufficient to bring them back over the Florida coast. The weather was worsening at Ft. Lauderdale and as the flight now seemed to be heading back to safety it was decided not to launch aircraft to the east to look for the missing flight.

At 17:50 the Gulf and Eastern Sea Frontier high frequency/DF nets had finally completed triangulation of bearings on FT-28 which produced a reliable fix on their location. They were within a 100-mile radius of 29°N, 79°W - north of the Bahamas and roughly 120 miles east of Daytona Beach. Unfortunately this information was not sent to Flight 19, probably because they already appeared to be heading in the right direction. The sun had set at 17:30 which meant that it would be dark before the flight reached land so all stations were alerted and instructed to turn on field lights/beacons and searchlights.

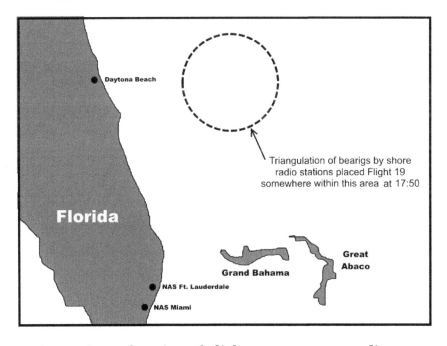

Approximate location of Flight 19 at 17:50 according to triangulation by shore radio stations. The area has a radius of 100 miles and the centre is 120 miles east of Daytona Beach.

But then at 18:04 another faint conversation between the

aircraft of Flight 19 was picked up:

> FT-28: *"Hello Powers, do you read me?"*
> FT-28: *"Hello Powers, this is Taylor. Do you read me? Over."*
> FT-36: *"Roger. I read you."*
> FT-28: *"Hello Powers. I have been trying to reach you."*
> FT-36: *"I thought you were calling base---"*
> FT-28: *"Negative. What course are we on?"*
> FT-36: *"Holding course 270."*
> FT-28: *"Affirmative. I am pretty sure we are over the Gulf of Mexico. We didn't go far enough east. How long have we been on this course?"*
> FT-36: *"About 45 minutes."*
> FT-28: *"I suggest we fly due east until we run out of gas. We have a better chance of being picked up close to shore. If we were near land we should be able to see a light or something. Are you listening? We may just as well turn around and go east again."*

It seemed that Taylor had handed control of Flight 19 to Captain Powers who was correctly leading them to the west. But, after just fifty minutes of flying in the right direction, Taylor was suggesting that they turn round and fly east once again, towards the open sea. It was no longer possible for

NHA3 to make radio contact with Flight 19 and at 18:20 a PBY Catalina flying boat was launched from the Dinner Key Coast Guard Air Station to try to contact the missing aircraft and to confirm their position and the direction they should fly to safety. Unfortunately, once it became airborne it was discovered that there was a fault in the PBY's radio equipment and it was unable to make contact with Flight 19. Radio messages from Flight 19 were increasingly garbled and difficult to understand. At around 18:30 the final clearly discernible radio message from Taylor was picked up by shore stations:

> *"All planes close up tight... we'll have to ditch unless landfall... when the first plane drops below 10 gallons, we all go down together."*

No further positively identified messages were heard from Flight 19 though NHA3 did pick up a very faint *"FT-3, FT-3, FT-3"* later. FT-3 was the aircraft flown by Ensign Joseph Bossi but despite repeated attempts, NHA3 was unable to raise any of the aircraft in Flight 19. A massive air/sea rescue operation was launched as soon as it was realized that the aircraft were not heading for shore and all stations were told to be on the look-out for the missing flight. The last possible sighting of Flight 19 was a radar contact by the aircraft carrier USS Solomons (CVE-67) at 19:00. The report from the Solomons which was included in the Board of Investigation report read:

> *"FOUR TO SIX PLANES - NO IFF - AT 1900 -*
> *LAT 2935 - LONG 8128   COURSE 170 -*
> *SPEED 120 - ESTIMATED ALTITUDE 4000*
> *FEET"*

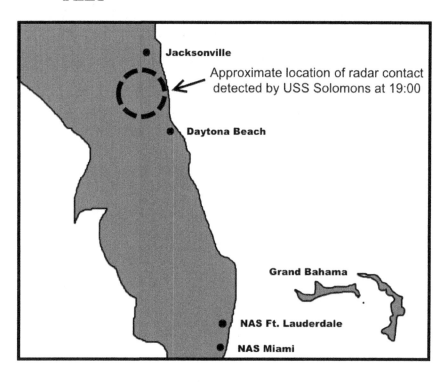

It has never been confirmed that the radar contact at 29°35'00.0"N, 81°28'00.0"W made by the USS Solomons was of Flight 19, though it certainly makes sense and the official Board of Investigation failed to find any other group of aircraft which might have accounted for this radar contact. If you compare the map above with the map showing the triangulated fix of Flight 19s position at 17:50, they are around 150 miles apart – a distance easily covered at the cruise speed of the TBM Avenger in that time. The altitude and speed of the radar contact are also what we would expect from Flight 19 and the course, heading almost due south, also makes sense in terms of aircraft which were trying to find an airbase at which to land. However, if this really was Flight 19, they must have been very close to running out of fuel at this point.

Search and rescue craft were launched all along the Florida coast to look for Flight 19. At the Banana River Naval Air Station near Jacksonville in Florida two giant Martin Mariner PBM-5 flying boats were launched to join the search at around 19:25. At 19:30 one of the aircraft, BuNo 59225, with 13 men onboard radioed in with a routine climb report. Nothing further was heard from this aircraft. At 20:00 a message was received from the *SS Gaines*, an oil tanker transiting the coast of Florida.

> *"At 1950hr observed a burst of flame, apparently an explosion, leaping flames 100ft high, and burning for 10min. Position 28°69'N, 8°25'W. At present passing through a big pool of oil. Circled area using searchlights, looking for survivors. None found."*

In a later message the Master of the *SS Gaines* confirmed that he had seen an aircraft catch fire and immediately crash, burning into the sea. The air search radar on the USS Solomons confirmed that they had been tracking two aircraft since they had taken off from Banana River NAS, but that one of the radar plots disappeared at around the time that SS Gaines reported seeing flames and an explosion. All on board the PBM-5 were presumed lost.

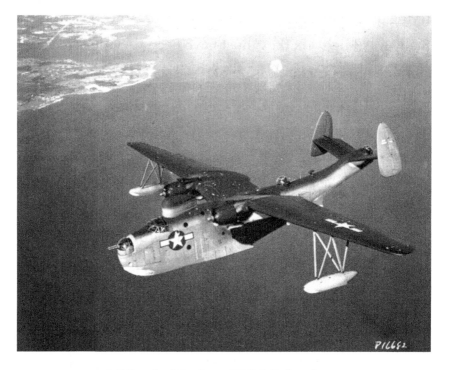

A Martin Mariner PBM flying boat

Photo: San Diego Air and Space Museum Archive

No wreckage of any of the six missing aircraft was found despite one of the largest search and rescue operations ever mounted. The only significant find during the search was a large oil slick at the location where *SS Gaines* had seen an aircraft come down. It was assumed that this was where the PBM-5 had crashed in to the sea but no other debris was seen. There was no trace of any of the missing aircraft from Flight 19.

On the following day the crew of an Eastern Air Lines DC-3 reported seeing a red flare in swampland in the vicinity of Sebastian, north of Vero Beach, Florida. This was followed up but no trace was found of any crashed aircraft.

A few days later the family of Sgt. George R. Paonessa, the radioman on one of the Flight 19 aircraft, received a Western Union telegram apparently sent from the Naval Air Station in Jacksonville. The telegram read: *"I am very much alive"* and was signed: *"Georgie"*. According to the family *"Georgie"* was how Sgt. Paonessa was known to close family members. No further communications were received by the family from *"Georgie"*.

Chapter 6: Everything looks wrong!

The US Navy Board of Investigation and the five hundred page report it produced into the loss of Flight 19 initially found Lt. Taylor guilty of *"mental aberration"* and blamed him for the loss of Flight 19. However his mother, Katherine Taylor, began her own investigation. The contention of Mrs Taylor and other members of the Taylor family was that, as the Navy was unable to prove exactly what had happened to Flight 19, it was unreasonable and unfair to place the blame for its loss solely upon Lt. Taylor. This was accepted by the US Navy and Taylor was exonerated in 1947 by the Board for Correction of Naval Records, in regard to *'responsibility for loss of lives and naval aircraft.'* The loss of Flight 19 was thereafter officially amended to *'cause unknown.'*

The story of the loss of Flight 19 would have probably been quietly forgotten had it not been for the frenzied wave of interest in the US on the subject of flying saucers (later to become the slightly more scientific sounding *'UFOs'*) and aliens which erupted in the late 1940s and early 1950s. When it became known that a US Air Force pilot had died when his aircraft crashed while he was investigating a sighting of a UFO, it was probably only a matter of time before someone looked at that *'cause unknown'* finding in the case of Flight 19 and wondered whether this too might have some connection with a more sinister cause for the loss of these six aircraft?

The first time this notion appeared in print was in 1952 in a short article in the October issue of Fate magazine titled *'Sea Mystery at Our Back Door'* and written by George X. Sand. The article hinted, without providing any rational explanation,that the loss of Flight 19 was somehow linked to other aircraft losses in the area and was caused by some unexplained and strange phenomena.

Ten years later, in the April 1962 issue of *American Legion* Magazine, Volume 72, Number 4, writer Allan W. Eckert published an article titled *'The Mystery of the Lost Patrol'*. This purported to be a detailed and factual discussion of the loss of Flight 19, but it was actually riddled with factual inaccuracies and invented dialogue. For example, it claimed that Flight 19 was a Coastal Defense System (CDS) patrol flight undertaken by trained crews and that Lt. Taylor's aircraft carried just two men while the others carried three each. This was the first time that anyone had referred to Flight 19 as a *'patrol'* (which was incorrect, it was a training flight) but the name stuck and many, many subsequent writers have called Flight 19 *'The Lost Patrol.'*

However, it was in quoting the supposed radio messages that Eckert's article descended into complete fiction. Some of the radio transmissions from Flight 19 were quoted in the article as:

> *"Calling tower, this an emergency, repeat, this is an emergency!"*

> *"We cannot be sure which way is west. We cannot be sure of any direction, everything looks wrong, strange, the ocean doesn't look as it should."*

And the final message from Flight 19 was given as:

> *"It is 16:25 hours. We are not certain where we are. Must be about 225 miles north-east of base. It looks like..."*

The article went on to explain that these messages were relayed by the pilots of Flight 19 with *'growing incredulity, fear and hysteria.'*

Now, if you have been paying attention, you'll realize that these radio messages are complete fakes which were never spoken by any of the pilots of the Flight 19 aircraft and to suggest that these men succumbed to *'fear and hysteria'* is to completely denigrate their memories – they may have been hopelessly lost, but there is no evidence that the pilots of Flight 19 ever acted with anything but professional calm. When Eckert was later challenged to provide a source for these new radio messages, he claimed that he *'couldn't remember'* where he had got them from.

The article went on to explain that the sea state was *'unusually mild'*, and implied that this should have allowed at least some of the aircraft to ditch safely (the sea state was actually very rough, and anyway, attempting to safely ditch an aircraft in the dark is virtually impossible in any sea state). The article also said that the Board of Investigation report noted that *'We are not even able to make a good guess as to what happened.'* It didn't – the original Board of Investigation report blamed Lt. Taylor and this was later amended to *'cause unknown'* only after pressure from the Taylor family. There was nothing in the Board of Investigation report into the loss of Flight 19 (or, I suspect, in any other Board of Investigation report) as to *'guesses'* about what happened.

In almost every respect, this article was invented, muddled or just plain wrong in what it said regarding the loss of Flight 19. The article also attempted to link the loss of Flight

19 with the later losses of two British civilian airliners. It described the disappearance of the Star Tiger and the Star Ariel, Avro Tudor airliners operated by British South American Airways and lost while en-route to Jamaica in 1948 and 1949 respectively, as '*similar incidents*' without in any way attempting to justify this. It also hinted at something strange in the Bermuda/Bahamas area which was somehow responsible for the mysterious disappearance of aircraft, though it wasn't able to suggest just what this might be.

This article may have been utter nonsense, but it was considerably more exciting than the rather dry conclusion of the Board of Investigation that Flight 19 simply got lost. This wouldn't be the last time that a writer would invent material to make the Flight 19 story sound more exciting and, as is so often the case, many subsequent writers simply assumed that this was an accurate report of what happened and adopted it as part of the Flight 19 story.

Chapter 7: Into the Bermuda Triangle

One of the first people to take the ideas of George Sand and Allan Eckert even further was the writer Vincent H. Gaddis who published an article in the February 1964 issue of Argosy magazine with the snappy title: *The Deadly Bermuda Triangle.* This is, as far as I am aware, the first time that anyone had used the term *'Bermuda Triangle'* in print.

In this, Gaddis freely quoted the spurious radio transmissions from Eckert's article and *'facts'* from that piece such as the notion that Flight 19 was a CDS patrol. However, he also added his own fictional extras including a supposed quote from a member of the Board of

Investigation who said of Flight 19: '*They vanished as completely as if they had flown to Mars.*'

Gaddis then went on to note that something must have affected all the compasses in the aircraft in Flight 19 at the same time, causing them to fly in a circle because otherwise '*they would have flown straight and seen land somewhere*'. It would have taken perhaps five minutes of looking at the actual events of 5th December to realize that this was utterly untrue but instead Gaddis went on to speculate that this same strange something that affected the compasses may also have caused the aircraft radios to malfunction (though there is no evidence they ever did) and to have made the sea look strange and the sun to be invisible (though these things are only noted in the invented radio messages in Eckert's article). Finally, he attributes these things which didn't actually happen to a strange '*atmospheric aberration*' which he goes on to describe as '*a hole in the sky.*'

Gaddis article, like Eckhart's, is almost completely inaccurate, muddled and plain wrong in what it says about Flight 19, but that didn't stop people latching on the idea of a strange place called the Bermuda Triangle which had, according to Gaddis '*destroyed hundreds of ships and planes without a trace.*'

Gaddis followed-up this article with a book, *Invisible Horizons*, published in 1965. In chapter 13, '*The Triangle of*

Death', this amplified the notion of the Bermuda Triangle and once again attributed the loss of Flight 19 to some strange and possibly even paranormal power in that area.

In 1969 the first book entirely about the Bermuda Triangle, *Limbo of the Lost*, was published by John Spencer. Spencer, keen to include as many disappearances as possible to bolster the sinister reputation of the Bermuda Triangle, included such disparate locations such as the Gulf of Mexico and New Jersey in his version of the fated area (which was now beginning to look like the '*Bermuda Blob*', but I guess that wasn't a title that would sell many books).

Then in 1974 the Bermuda Triangle finally broke through into the mainstream. Charles Frambach Berlitz published the seminal book *The Bermuda Triangle* which went on to sell over five million copies and suddenly everyone had heard of the Bermuda Triangle.

Charles Berlitz was grandson of the founder of the world famous Berlitz School of Languages. In the late 1960s he sold the company to publishing firm Crowell, Collier & Macmillan so that he could focus on writing about the things that really interested him: Atlantis, ancient astronauts and the visitation of the earth by extraterrestrials.

Charles Berlitz wrote popular non-fiction books, but only if you are willing to take a very broad view of that term. In *The Bermuda Triangle*, he explained that the loss of Flight 19 and other aircraft and ships in the same area was almost certainly due to the actions of nasty extraterrestrials, possibly using power crystals retrieved from ancient Atlantis or by controlling vortices from the fourth dimension. Berlitz wasn't above twisting accounts to make them better fit his whacky theories or to simply inventing evidence if nothing suitable existed.

To the spurious radio messages already invented by Eckert, Berlitz added more which were claimed to have come from Flight 19 including:

"We're entering white water..."

And my personal favorite:

"Don't come after us. They look like they're from outer space!"

When Berlitz was later asked to provide the source of these dramatic radio messages, he claimed that they had come from hand-written notes provided to him by one of the people who was present at NAS Ft. Lauderdale on the day that Flight 19 vanished, Commander R.H. Wishing. However, a BBC documentary crew were later able to interview Commander Wishing who said that he had never kept handwritten notes of radio communications and anyway, he hadn't been on duty on 5th December 1945.

Thanks to the popularity of Berlitz' book, these radio messages and the notion that there was an extraterrestrial element in the disappearance of Flight 19 have taken root in the popular imagination and are often quoted to support paranormal explanations for this event.

Books and articles about the Bermuda Triangle and its role in the disappearance of Flight 19 have continued to appear. As recently as 2016 a book called *The Bermuda Triangle: Unexplained Disappearances Beneath the Waves* by Cheryl Leonard was published. It has this to say about Flight 19:

> *'On December 5, 1945, a training flight of TBM Avenger bombers of the US Navy known as Flight 19, were 14 men who went missing while flying over the Atlantic.'*

Wow! Charles Berlitz may have been a crazy dingbat who occasionally made things up when it suited him, but reading this particular book is a reminder that he could at least write a coherent sentence.

You see, there is one important thing that anyone discussing the Bermuda Triangle should bear in mind: It doesn't exist. The idea of the Bermuda Triangle was invented by unscrupulous writers in order to sell magazines and books. All the incidents attributed by these writers to mysterious forces were actually caused by bad weather or accidents, or they happened far from the supposed area of the triangle or both or (in a few cases) they never happened at all.

My research suggests very strongly that the loss of Flight 19 has nothing to do with the Bermuda Triangle, aliens, UFOs, giant waterspouts, power crystals from Atlantis or *'holes in the sky.'* Sorry. I'm sure this book would sell better if it did but, unlike some writers, I'm not willing to make this stuff up. And if you really believe the contention apparently seriously quoted in some websites that the alleged UFO seen floating in space by the crew of Apollo 11 in 1969 is actually one of the missing Flight 19 aircraft then I can only suggest that you try lying quietly in a darkened room with a damp cloth on your head to see if that helps you to feel any better.

There is no doubt that the seas off the East coast of the US can be a dangerous place (though the maritime accident records of Lloyd's of London show that they are no more dangerous than many other congested sea lanes elsewhere in the world). However, the reasons are physical rather than paranormal. The Gulf Stream is swift and turbulent in this area, leading to unpredictable weather including sudden localized thunderstorms and fog. The ocean floor is very varied here, with deep trenches, shallow shoals and reefs. This can lead to unpredictable sea conditions and the interaction of currents with the ocean floor can change existing shoals or even create new ones in an astonishingly short period of time. But, I don't think that there is any evidence whatsoever that any of these things are directly related to the loss of Flight 19.

.

Chapter 8: Meanwhile, back in the real world...

Now that we have consigned the Bermuda Triangle to the hole in the sky in which it rightly belongs, let's get back to looking at the search for real evidence about what happened to Flight 19.

The initial search for the missing aircraft was massive, involving over two hundred aircraft and ships and continuing for five days. Other than an oil slick which might have marked the spot where the Mariner PBM-5 crashed into the sea, it found no wreckage, liferafts or any trace of any of the missing aircraft.

The telegram received by the family of Sgt. George R. Paonessa on the 10th December was also extensively investigated. Although the name of the sender of the telegram was given as '*Georgie*', and it was confirmed that this was how Sgt. Paonessa was known within the family, it was also revealed that the Sgt. was also known as '*Georgie*' to some navy colleagues, so this might have been widely known. No other communications were received from '*Georgie*' and there was no attempt, for example, to access bank accounts owned by Sgt. Paonessa. Investigators finally concluded that there was no real evidence that Sgt.

Paonessa was still alive and that the telegram was a cruel hoax.

The red flare reported by the crew of a an Eastern Air Lines DC-3 in swampland near the city of Sebastian in Indian River County in Florida led to a number of searches of the area by low-flying navy aircraft in the days following the disappearance of Flight 19, but none spotted any debris or located a crash site. However, in 1963 Graham Stikelether, an Indian River County attorney who later became a judge, was hunting in swampland about eight miles southwest of Sebastian when he found the wreckage of what appeared to be a single-engine naval aircraft. The aircraft contained the remains of two bodies and Stikelether notified the Navy and the aircraft and human remains were retrieved.

Stikelether claimed that he was initially told that the aircraft was one of those from Flight 19, but naval authorities later denied this. Stikelether was curious about the identities of the bodies he had discovered so he called a friend in the Pentagon and asked if he could help. Stikelether claimed that the friend later called back and strongly advised him to 'just drop it.' Stikelether made no further attempt to identify the aircraft he had found until 1989 when he read an article on missing warplanes in Omni magazine written by aviation researcher and ex-military helicopter pilot Jon Myhre.

Stikelether contacted Myhre and told him of the discovery in 1963. Myhre was interested in the story of Flight 19 and believed that the location identified by Stikelether was a plausible crash site for an aircraft from Flight 19 if the radar sighting by the USS Solomons was of the missing aircraft. However, bizarrely, the US navy has consistently refused to identify the bodies or the aircraft found by Stikelether in 1963. When Myhre first contacted the Navy, he was told that, unless he provided the precise date on which the wreck was found, no information would be released. Stikelether no longer remembered the exact date, so this temporarily prevented further enquiries. Graham Stikelether died in 2009 but, in 2013, Myhre submitted a federal Freedom of Information request for information about the crashed aircraft.

He received no information on the identities in response to this request and an un-named federal employee told him that the identities of the crash victims had been redacted from the Navy accident report and were thus exempt from the FOI request. In January 2018, Myhre appealed directly to Admiral Samuel Cox, director of the Naval History and Heritage Command, and asked for his help in identifying the remains found by Stikelether in 1963. Heritage Command media spokesman Paul Taylor later told a local newspaper that this would be very difficult because the

Navy could not find any documentation which identified the dead men. He said: *"The Navy still doesn't have enough information to determine who they were. There are no relevant records to answer his question, but we'll continue to work the case."*

The seeming reluctance on the part of the US Navy to identify the bodies discovered by Graham Stikelether is very odd. It's not that they didn't know who these men were, it appears that the relevant records were later deliberately redacted from the accident report. Stikelether was adamant that the crashed aircraft contained only two bodies, which has led to speculation that this was the aircraft flown by US Marine Corps Captain Edward Powers and that the other body was that of Sgt. Howell Thompson, the gunner. The third crewman of this aircraft was radioman Sgt. George R. Paonessa. Perhaps, some people wondered, Paonessa really did survive to send a telegram to his family and, for completely unknown reasons, the US Navy choose to conceal the identities of the other two bodies when the wreck was found? It's an interesting theory, but it must remain nothing more than speculation until the aircraft and the human remains found in 1963 are finally and positively identified by the US Navy.

In May 1989, at around the same time that Graham Stikelether was reading the article in Omni about Flight 19, a brush fire broke out in swampland in Broward County, Florida near a stretch of the I-75 Highway known as Alligator Alley. A Broward County Sherriff's deputy was flying a helicopter near the scene of the fire when he spotted aircraft wreckage around ten miles west of the Alligator Alley toll booth and about one mile north of the I-75. The wreck had previously been concealed by scrub and long grass and had only become visible when the fire exposed the crash site.

Initial investigations showed that this was a TBM-3 Avenger, the same type of aircraft flown by Charles Taylor in Flight 19. Navy records were consulted and the only TBM-3 listed as missing between 1944 and 1952 was the aircraft flown by Taylor. A rubber heel found in the wreck was found to have come from a size 11 or 12 dress shoe, most likely worn by a man of at least six feet tall – Charles Taylor was 6' 1" tall. Excitement mounted as it seemed more and more likely that this was the flight leader's aircraft from Flight 19.

It took a number of years to finally prove that Navy records were misleading and this wasn't an aircraft from Flight 19 at all. Instead, this TBM-3 had been flown in March 1947 by a Naval Reserve Officer, Ensign Ralph Wachob, on a navigational flight from Miami to Tampa when he flew into bad weather, lost control of the aircraft, crashed and was killed. A US Navy search and rescue team found the crash site and recovered Ensign Wachob's body soon after the accident, but there was no attempt to recover the wrecked aircraft. Because the crashed aircraft had been located, it wasn't listed as missing in US Navy records which inadvertently fuelled initial speculation that this might have been one of the aircraft from Flight 19.

Also in 1989 Jon Myhre and a group of salvage experts who called themselves Project 19 funded the recovery of the wreck of a TBM-1C aircraft which had been located in four hundred feet of water off the coast of Florida, not far from Cape Canaveral. Myhre believed that this might be aircraft FT-117 from flight 19, but a lengthy investigation finally proved that it was an Avenger from NAS Miami and nothing to do with Flight 19.

Then, in May 1991, the Deep See, a high-tech salvage ship that was searching for sunken Spanish treasure ships off the coast of Florida made a sensational discovery: it found five Avenger aircraft in 600 feet of water around ten miles northwest of Ft. Lauderdale. A videotape was released which showed the five aircraft sitting eerily on the seabed within one mile of each other. Even their cockpits and turrets were intact and Graham Hawkes, project director of Scientific Search Project, the company who operated the Deep See excitedly told reporters: "*We've seen some pretty strange sights on the ocean floor, but it was with amazement and disbelief that we saw this. I think we've put one of aviation's greatest mysteries very much to rest."*

The video tape even appeared to show faint markings on one of the aircraft that appeared to be the number '28', the number of the aircraft flown by Charles Taylor. The discovery was made public when lawyers for Scientific Search Project filed suit in federal court in Miami seeking title to the five aircraft – the company believed that they might be worth millions of dollars to museums if they were the aircraft from Flight 19 and if they could be recovered.

U.S. District Judge Kenneth Ryskamp granted the company temporary possession and a salvage operation was conducted amid frenzied publicity and in front of a film crew from the *Unsolved Mysteries* TV show. On August 13th 1991, one of the Avengers discovered by the Deep See was finally recovered from the seabed. To the disappointment of almost everyone, it was quickly proved not to be one of the Flight 19 aircraft and subsequent investigation proved that none of the wrecks located by the Deep See had anything to do with Flight19.

Instead, the recovered aircraft was found to from NAS Miami, though how it or any of the other four Avengers located by the Deep See came to be six hundred feet down in the ocean off Ft. Lauderdale provides another as yet unsolved aviation mystery.

Photo: Richard C. Drew

To date, no physical trace of any aircraft that was in Flight 19 has been found. There remains a question about the identity of the aircraft and bodies discovered by Graham Stikelether in 1963 but there is currently no firm evidence that this was one of the missing aircraft.

Chapter 9: Lt. Charles Taylor

The location of wreckage of one or more of the Flight 19 aircraft would certainly help to solve part of this mystery. However, to date no crash site has been definitely identified as belonging to any of these aircraft and no hard evidence of any kind has been found. In the absence of such evidence, is there any other way to assess just what happened to Flight 19 and the Mariner flying boat which was sent to search for them?

Any attempt to analyze what happened to Flight 19 on 5th December 1945 must focus on the actions of the flight leader, Lt. Charles Taylor. But, as soon as you start to research this topic, it becomes clear that surprisingly little is known about the man at the centre of one of the most enduring aviation mysteries.

Charles Carroll Taylor was born in October 1917, in Nueces County, Texas and he graduated from Texas A&M University. He joined the US Naval Reserve in 1941 and graduated as a pilot from NAS Corpus Christi in February 1942. He flew with Scouting Squadron 62 until November 1943, operating out of NAS Miami and flying anti-submarine patrols over the Florida Keys and the Gulf of Mexico. He also became a flight instructor during this time. He then became a pilot with Torpedo Squadron 7, the Strike

Eagles. From April 1944 to December 1944 he served on the Essex class aircraft carrier USS Hancock (CV-19) and saw combat as part of as part of Task Force 38 in attacks on shipping and shore targets on and around the island of Okinawa.

He then spent time as a Flight Instructor at NAS Miami with Squadron 79 and on November 21st, 1945, he was transferred to NAS Ft. Lauderdale as part of a large-scale transfer of personnel to take up duties as a Flight Instructor there. Before taking-off with Flight 19 Taylor had logged a total of over 2,500 flight hours with 616 of those in Avengers. The records show that he made his first familiarization flight from NAS Ft. Lauderdale on 1st December. We can't be certain, but it is likely that Flight 19 on December 5th was the first training flight he had taken up since arriving and perhaps only his second flight from NAS Ft. Lauderdale.

It's clear that Charles Taylor was an experienced pilot who had seen combat and, though he had been transferred to Ft. Lauderdale less than three weeks before the fatal flight, he had previously flown out of Miami, only twenty miles away, and he should have been very familiar with landmarks and weather conditions in the area.

Lt. Taylor seems to have been generally well regarded by

other personnel he served with. The gunner and radioman he had flown with on the USS Hancock during the war described him as an excellent pilot and the perfect southern gentleman who was also proud to be a U.S. Navy aviator. However, some colleagues described Taylor as a loner and a man who wasn't particularly interested in flying or the navy. It was suggested that the only reason he stayed in the navy after the war ended was because he didn't know what else to do (and there weren't many jobs available that called for a navy aviator's skills and experience).

Lt. Charles Carroll Taylor

Although photographs show the tall, slim Taylor to have been a very handsome man, he didn't seem particularly interested in women and didn't appear to have made any close friends during his time at either NAS Miami or NAS Ft. Lauderdale. When author Larry Kusche spent time in the late 1970s researching for his book *The Disappearance of Flight 19*, he sought out and interviewed several of Taylor's colleagues from the navy. However, it is notable that none of these men seemed to know Taylor well and none were able to provide any useful insight into his personality.

It's also worth noting that, although Taylor was described by the majority of his fellow fliers as a reliable and careful airman, he had been forced to ditch in the sea twice since qualifying as a pilot in 1942. On each occasion this had resulted from his getting lost rather than being caused by combat damage or enemy action.

On June 14th, 1944, near Trinidad, Taylor '*lost his bearings*' (according to the gunner in his aircraft) and was forced to ditch in the Pacific when he ran out of fuel, though fortunately he and his crew were quickly rescued. On January 30th, 1945 Taylor was unable to find his landing field on Guam. He flew in the wrong direction, out of radio contact with his landing field, and was forced to ditch in the ocean again when he ran out of fuel. This time, he and his crewman spent more than twenty-four uncomfortable hours adrift in a rubber raft before being rescued and given thirty days survivor's leave to recover. Taylor was not officially censured for either incident, but it's notable that he had become so seriously lost on two previous occasions that he had not been able to make it back to base.

We do know that something was wrong with Charles Taylor on 5th December. The official Board of Investigation report notes that he arrived at the base late at 13:10 and that, instead of joining his trainees, he went immediately to see the Aviation Duty Officer, Lt. Arthur Curtis, and asked to be excused from leading Flight 19. We don't know why, or if he asked to be excused all flying or just from leading Flight 19. The Navy report after the incident only notes that when asked for a reason, he *declined to give one.* He was told by Lt. Curtis that no replacement training pilot was available and that he would therefore have to lead Flight 19.

I think we can safely assume that this is a carefully circumspect navy account of what actually happened. For an assigned training officer to arrive late and then ask to be excused a scheduled training flight at such short notice is very unusual, and I don't believe for a moment that the officer involved would simply accept Taylor's refusal to give a reason and send him out on the flight without asking more questions. In particular, the idea that Curtis didn't try to press Taylor for his reasons for not wanting to fly seems unlikely. He might have been ill or suffering from some physical impairment which would have prevented him from flying.

The official Navy version sounds like, at the very least, an oversimplification. It's also notable that official US Navy policy is that no-one will be forced to fly in any circumstances. Any US Navy pilot can refuse to fly at any time (though they will likely find that are no longer US Navy pilots if they do so). In this context, Taylor obviously didn't forcefully refuse to fly that day – he must have asked if a replacement was available, and when told that there wasn't, he agreed to fly.

There is nothing else in the Board of Investigation report to give any clues to Taylor's state of mind but there were unconfirmed rumors from other personnel on the base that he was suffering from a monumental hangover on December 5th after over-indulging at the Officer's Club the night before. However, personnel who saw him when he arrived at Ft. Lauderdale on 5th December (including Lt. Willard Stoll, the lead pilot of Flight 18 who spoke to Taylor in the briefing room) said that he seemed entirely normal and showed no signs of distress or illness.

It was also claimed by Taylor's room-mate in the Officer's Quarters at NAS Ft. Lauderdale that he had received a letter that morning which seemed to upset him. When asked about the letter, Taylor simply said that he was fine and tucked it inside his flight jacket without saying who it was from or what it was about.

Perhaps Charles Taylor did give Lt. Curtis a reason for not wanting to fly, but it wasn't accepted? Perhaps there was an extended discussion or even an argument? We'll never know for sure, and speculating probably isn't helpful, but we do know that for some unknown reason, Charles Taylor didn't want to be the lead pilot for Flight 19 on December 5th.

The next issue is whether Charles Taylor had a wristwatch when he flew as lead in Flight 19? He must have known that the aircraft he would be flying that day was unlikely to have a clock. A dead-reckoning exercise like Navigation Problem Number 1 requires that the course and speed of the aircraft is known at all times, and that these are used with elapsed time to calculate just where you are. A pilot who doesn't know how long he has been flying on a particular course will be lost as soon as he is out of sight of land. In the case of a training flight, it's imperative that the experienced instructor knows the location of the flight at all times, so that he can guide the flight back on course if a trainee gets lost.

But, in several of the radio transmissions logged between the aircraft of Flight 19, Taylor is heard to ask how long they have been on a particular course? This strongly suggests that he wasn't able to monitor the time himself and therefore cannot have been wearing a wristwatch. Did he forget to bring his watch or did he leave it behind because he assumed that he wouldn't be flying that day? Did he assume that, because another pilot would be flying the lead on each leg of the exercise, he wouldn't be required to do any navigation himself? If any of these things are true, they seem to imply a dangerously casual attitude towards his duties as an instructor pilot on the part of Lt. Taylor.

Then there are the radio messages which provide strong clues that Charles Taylor was, at the very least, suffering from extreme mental confusion. Take, for example, the following transmission to Lt. Cox in FT-74 at 15:50:

> *"Both my compasses are out and I am trying to find Fort Lauderdale, Florida. I am over land but it's broken. I am sure I'm in the Keys but I don't know how far down and I don't know how to get to Fort Lauderdale."*

There are several interesting points here. The first is *"Both my compasses are out"*. It would be very unusual indeed in an aircraft such as the Avenger to simultaneously have both compasses stop working. These were pre-electronic days and the compasses fitted to the TBM were entirely separate mechanical devices. It's difficult to imagine anything short of major combat damage that could have caused both to fail simultaneously. Taylor obviously felt that he couldn't trust his compasses, but was this due to his mental state rather than a mechanical failure? Next *"I am over land but it's broken"*. Wherever Taylor was at 15:50, he was within sight of land, which may help us to work out where he was. But the most astonishing thing he says is *"I'm sure I'm in the Keys, but I don't know how far down and I don't know how to get to Fort Lauderdale."* There are two separate things here we need to consider. The first is that Taylor seems to believe that the broken land he is looking at is part of the Florida Keys.

This is so completely bonkers that it suggests that Taylor was suffering at this point from some sort of major mental breakdown – although the small islands of the Bahama Cays and the Florida keys look fairly similar from the air, at 15:50 Flight 19 was a very long way east of the Keys. Taylor must have known this, and it makes no sense at all for him to think that the flight has suddenly been transported more than one hundred miles to the west.

The second notable thing about this transmission is perhaps even more important - if the flight really was over the Florida Keys as Taylor seemed to believe, then getting to NAS Ft. Lauderdale should have been easy. All that would have been necessary would have been to fly north following the Keys until they reached Florida. Even without a compass, all you have to do to fly north in the Keys in the afternoon is to put the sun on your port wing, something every pilot flying out of NAS Miami and NAS Ft. Lauderdale was aware of. But Taylor, who had spent a fair part of his career as a naval pilot flying over the Keys, tells Cox that he doesn't know how to get to NAS Ft. Lauderdale and he can't tell which way is north. To suggest that an experienced pilot who was over the Florida Keys didn't know how to get to NAS Ft. Lauderdale is even more surprising than Taylor's initial error of location.

At this point, it seems that something was very wrong with Lt. Taylor's powers of reasoning. This seems to be confirmed by the preceding transmissions overheard between Captain Powers and Lieutenant Taylor where Taylor seems to be questioning the direction in which Powers is leading the flight. Yet, just a few minutes later Taylor tells Cox that both his compasses are out so how could he have known that the heading on which Powers was flying was wrong?

If we add this to Taylor's initial inability to remember his own radio call-sign (he first identified himself to Cox as 'MT-28' rather than 'FT-28'), it certainly appears that he was suffering from some sort of mental issues though we have no idea of whether these were a result of fatigue, a hangover or something else entirely. However, in any attempt to rationally analyze what happened to Flight 19, it's very important to keep in mind the fact that the evidence strongly suggests that Charles Taylor wasn't thinking rationally on the afternoon of December 5th.

Chapter 10: The Real Story of Flight 19

The five aircraft of Flight 19 took off from one of the three main runways at NAS Ft. Lauderdale at approximately 14:10. They formed up and were then seen to fly off to the east.

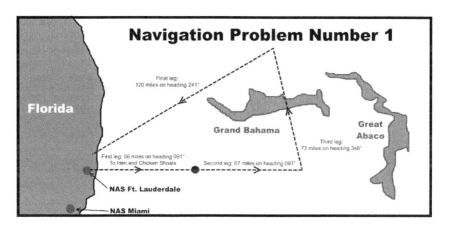

Navigation Problem Number 1

The first waypoint on their navigation exercise was Hen and Chicken Shoals, fifty-six miles from NAS Ft. Lauderdale. Flight 19 should have arrived at this location soon after 14:30, and this seems to be confirmed by the two radio messages discussing the dropping of bombs that were logged by the NAS Ft. Lauderdale Operations Center between 14:30 and 15:00. The Board of Investigation report also noted that a fishing boat in the vicinity of Hen and Chicken Shoals reported seeing 'three or four' aircraft heading east at about 15:00. No other Navy aircraft were in this vicinity, so this must have been Flight 19, heading for their next turning point and apparently on-schedule.

The next leg of the navigation exercise required Flight 19 to fly east for a further sixty-seven miles until they reached Great Stirrup Cay, something that should have taken around twenty-five minutes. Sometime around 15:30 they should have arrived at the turning point and turned towards the north to overfly the large island of Grand Bahama.

However, the next time that anyone heard from Flight 19 was at 15:40 when Lt. Cox overheard Captain Powers in aircraft FT-36 say, apparently to Charles Taylor: *"I don't know where we are. We must have got lost after that last turn."*

So, it would appear that Flight 19 had reached their second waypoint and turning point at Great Stirrup Cay, but that something had gone wrong after they had made the turn, leading them to believe that they were off-course. But, at 15:40 when the radio transmission from Powers was overheard, they were probably less than fifteen minutes and forty miles from their turning point over Great Stirrup Cay. So, while there might have been some doubt about the heading on which they were currently flying, they must still have known the approximate area that they were in.

Yet, as Lt. Cox listened to an exchange between the pilots of

Flight 19, at around 15:50 he heard one of the other pilots, presumably Taylor, say "*I think we must be over the Keys.*" When Cox made radio contact with Flight 19 a short time later, Taylor confirmed his belief that they were over the Florida Keys. Somehow and in some way that we don't understand, Charles Taylor had mentally transposed his position over one hundred and fifty miles to the west. He was looking down at the small, broken islands of the Bahama Cays, which do indeed look similar to the Florida Keys, and he assumed that Flight 19 was south of Florida and perhaps in the Gulf of Mexico. This was completely impossible, but to Taylor it somehow seemed logical and everything that followed was based on this one, tragic failure of reasoning.

For the three hours that the aircraft remained in the air, all the actions Taylor took were consistent and sensible if Flight 19 had been in the Gulf of Mexico at 15:50. However, because the flight was actually somewhere over the Bahamas at 15:50, Taylor's actions were disastrously and catastrophically wrong and he consistently led the flight further from safety.

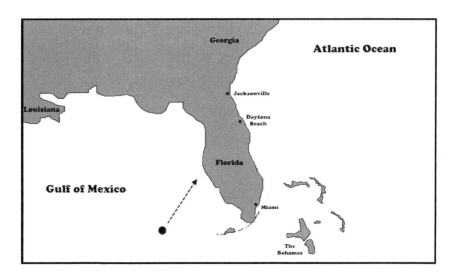

The black dot on the diagram above represents the approximate area in which Lt. Taylor seemed to <u>believe</u> Flight 19 was at around 16:00 (even though this was physically impossible). Within that context, his insistence that they fly north-east (arrowed) makes perfect sense because this would take them towards the coast of Florida.

This is an important point and it's worth stressing. Many people have tried to blame the loss of Flight 19 on compass problems, other equipment failures or even some sort of strange weather, but I don't think any of these are true. From the radio messages it is certainly clear that Taylor and Powers both had concerns about the reliability of their compasses. This has led to speculation about some kind of magnetic anomaly which led the flight astray. However, any pilot is trained to use the position of the sun as a guide to direction, and even when the sun is obscured by cloud, its general location is still clear. The subsequent problems for Flight 19 weren't caused because they didn't know the direction in which they were flying, their problems arose because they couldn't agree on which direction they <u>ought</u> to be flying.

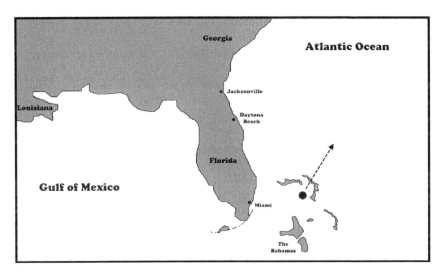

The black dot on the diagram above shows approximately where Flight 19 <u>actually was</u> at 16:00. Flying north-east (arrowed) as Taylor suggested would take them away from land and out over the Atlantic Ocean.

Following a compass course while flying over the ocean is only useful if you know where you are starting from. Lt. Taylor ordered Flight 19 to follow a course that took them generally to the north and east. If they had been, as he mistakenly believed, over the Gulf of Mexico, this would have brought them towards the coast of Florida and safety.

But because they were far to the east, it actually took them further out over the open ocean. Flight 19 was lost not because of compass problems or equipment failures but because their flight leader ordered them to fly in the wrong direction.

The Board of Investigation report into the loss of Flight 19 noted that Taylor: '...*allowed himself to be led to believe he was in a position in which he could not possibly have been.*' It went on to say:

> '*Approx 1600, radio messages were intercepted that led us to believe that this flight was lost in the vicinity of Bahama Is. Efforts were made immediately to contact this flight by radio and to direct them to fly a course of 270 degrees or into sun. If these directions had been heard and carried out, we are certain this flight would have returned to base safely.*
>
> *Training Dept has been directed to intensify training in lost plane procedure & stress with all pilots the necessity for carrying out correct procedure when lost.*'

The suggestion of some sort of magnetic or weather anomaly which led Flight 19 off course also seems unlikely because Flight 18, another flight of five Avenger aircraft from NAS Ft. Lauderdale, had taken off less than one hour before Flight 19 and that flight completed Navigation Problem Number 1 and returned to base safely. Their instructor and flight leader, Lt. Willard Stoll, reported no adverse or unusual conditions in the area.

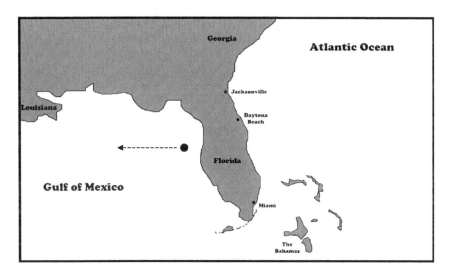

The black dot above shows approximately where Lt. Taylor seemed to <u>believe</u> Flight 19 was at around 17:00. This was when he was heard to say *"You didn't get far enough east!"* To him, the insistence of shore personnel and the other pilots of Flight 19 that they needed to fly west (arrowed) made no sense – this would just take them deeper into the Gulf of Mexico.

What occurred within Flight 19 was a tragic tug-of-war between personnel ashore and the four student pilots, who seemed to know approximately where Flight 19 was, and their instructor, who clearly did not. By five o'clock, approximately one and a quarter hours since Taylor had first become confused about their position, other pilots in the flight were heard to angrily say: *"Dammit, if we could just fly west we would get home"* and *"Hold it: head west, dammit!"* Taylor finally seemed to accept this because at 17:15, he broadcast to the Air-Sea Rescue Task Unit Four at Port Everglades: *"We will fly 270 degrees until we hit the beach or run out of gas."*

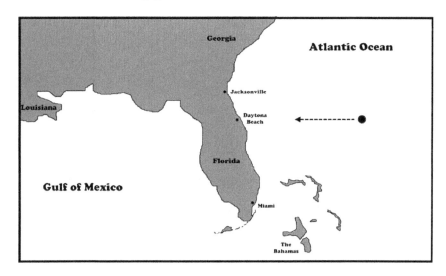

The black dot on the diagram above shows approximately where Flight 19 <u>actually was</u> at 17:00. Flying west (arrowed) would take them towards Florida and safety.

At that point, everyone ashore must have breathed a sigh of relief. It appeared that Flight 19 was finally heading west, in the right direction. They were known to have had more than two hours of fuel left and, although it would be dark when they reached land, all Naval Air Stations were told to switch on searchlights, beacons and runway lights to allow the flight to land safely. At 17:50, triangulation of radio signals from Flight 19 confirmed that they were somewhere east of Daytona Beach in Florida and that, if they continued to fly west, they would reach safety.

Then, horrifically, at 18:04, the Air-Sea Rescue Task Unit Four at Port Everglades picked up a faint radio transmission from Charles Taylor in Flight 19:

> *"I suggest we fly due east until we run out of gas. We have a better chance of being picked up close to shore. If we were near land we should be able to see a light or something. Are you listening? We may just as well turn around and go east again."*

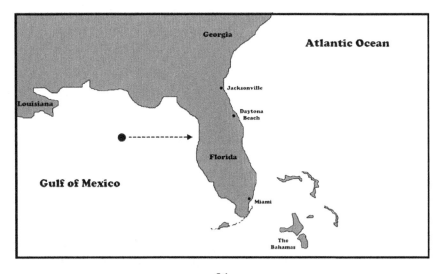

The black dot above shows approximately where Lt. Taylor seemed to <u>believe</u> Flight 19 was at around 18:00. He wanted them to turn around and fly east (arrowed), which he thought would take them towards the coast of Florida.

So, at this point they were still flying west, towards safety, but Taylor wanted the flight to turn around and head back to the east. Taylor clearly still mistakenly thought that they were somewhere over the Gulf of Mexico. This radio message also provides another clue to Taylor's increasing mental dissociation. The flight had been flying west for fifty minutes. During that time they have not sighted land. If they turned round and flew back the way they had come, they knew they wouldn't see land for at least fifty minutes, by which time they would be critically low on fuel. Whatever the answer was at this point, it wasn't turning round and going back the same way they had just come, and yet that's what Taylor was suggesting.

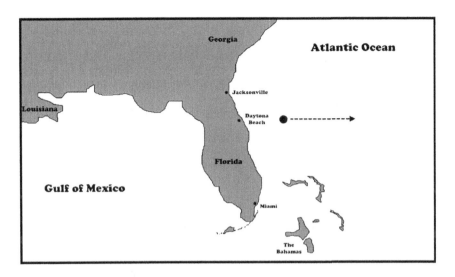

The black dot on the diagram above shows approximately where Flight 19 <u>actually</u> was at 18:00, confirmed by triangulation of their radio broadcasts. Flying east (arrowed) would take them further out into the Atlantic Ocean.

That transmission at 18:04 is the last piece of evidence we have of the course which Flight 19 was following. Only one further faint radio message was received by the Air-Sea Rescue Task Unit Four at Port Everglades and that didn't say anything about what course they were flying. We don't know for certain whether after 18:04 Flight 19 continued to fly to the west and towards Florida or whether they took Taylor's advice and headed back to the east, ditching somewhere in the Atlantic when they finally ran out of fuel.

There is one further possible clue. The radar sighting by the

USS Solomons at 19:00 is mentioned in the official Board of Investigation report but for some reason it has often been ignored by Flight 19 researchers. It's certainly likely that Flight 19 was still in the air at 19:00 – they took off at 14:10 with full tanks of fuel which should have kept them in the air for 5 - 5½ hours. Navy investigators later estimated that, with careful management of fuel, it might have been possible for Flight 19 to continue flying until as late as 19:50.

The radar contact was of a group of *'four to six planes'* and Navy investigators who compiled the Board of Investigation report stated that no other groups of aircraft were known to be in the area at the time. The speed is right for Avengers – the radar report estimated 120knots and the standard cruising speed of the Avenger is 135 knots but it makes sense to fly more slowly if you're trying to conserve fuel. The contact sighting also noted *'Estimated altitude 4000 feet'*. In his earlier transmissions Taylor noted that he was at *'Angels 3.5'* or 3,500 feet and later at 4,500 feet. Finally the course is 170°, almost due south. You'll recall that the original flight plan for Flight 19 required them to turn to the south once they crossed the coast of Florida in order to find NAS Ft. Lauderdale.

But if this was Flight 19, what happened to them after that? The USS Solomons radar sighting put them over land, somewhere in a triangle formed by Daytona Beach to the south, St. Augustine to the north and Gainesville to the west. It's a desolate area of swampland and rivers and by 19:00 on the 5th December the weather had closed in with huge seas and a large area of turbulent air rolling out of a storm centered over Georgia. Forty miles-per-hour winds were recorded at 1,000 feet and full hurricane force winds of over 75 miles an hour were recorded at Jacksonville at 16:00 at 8,000 feet. Rescue aircraft later described the cloudbase as 800 – 1200 feet.

So, it was dark, stormy and at 4,000 feet any aircraft in the position plotted by the USS Solomons would have been in the clouds and unable to see the ground or the lights of Daytona Beach or Gainesville in the distance. If this was indeed Flight 19, they were still in big trouble and they may not even have realized that they were over land.

This has led many Flight 19 researchers to believe that the aircraft crashed somewhere in Florida. However, there is one very strong reason to think that this radar contact could not have been the aircraft of Flight 19. No radio transmissions were picked up by the Air-Sea Rescue Task Unit Four at Port Everglades or any of the other stations desperately monitoring the airwaves for clues about the location of Flight 19 after their last transmission at 18:30. The last radio message was described as being very faint indeed, suggesting that the aircraft were far out over the Atlantic. It makes no sense that Flight 19 could have been picked up on radar over land just thirty minutes later. It's also impossible to understand how the radio messages which must have been continually passing between the aircraft of the flight as they ran low on fuel would not have been picked up by multiple listening stations if Flight 19 really was over Florida at 19:00.

The complete absence of logged radio transmissions makes me inclined to strongly doubt that the radar contact reported by the USS Solomons really was the aircraft of Flight 19. I can't explain what it was – some sort of weather-related anomaly perhaps, or even another group of aircraft, but the lack of radio transmissions mean that I don't believe that it could have been Flight 19.

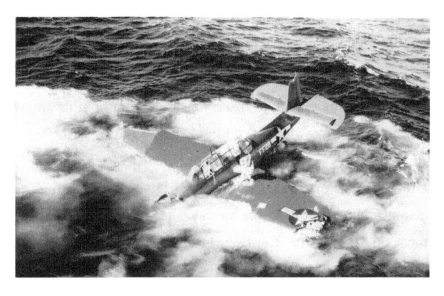

I think it much more likely that the aircraft of Flight 19 acceded to the suggestion of their experienced instructor and turned to the east sometime after 18:30. I think they then ditched in darkness somewhere in the Atlantic Ocean between 19:00 and 19:50 when they became critically low on fuel. By that time, the winds were severe, seas were running very high indeed and the chances of anyone surviving a ditching even in daylight were miniscule. At night, former TBM pilots have confirmed that there was no chance at all.

I suspect that all the aircraft of Flight 19 broke up as they struck the unyielding water and that the men on-board died immediately. Rough seas and strong winds meant that any debris remaining on the surface would have been broken up and dispersed well before search aircraft scoured the area the following morning.

For these reasons, I don't believe that any of the men of Flight 19 survived and I think that the telegram received by George R. Paonessa's family was nothing more than a particularly cruel practical joke. However, it may be worth mentioning that at the Arlington National Cemetery in Virginia there is only one headstone for any member of Flight 19 and that is for Sgt. Paonessa. The cemetery administration claim that they do not know when the stone was placed there or who paid for it, but they have confirmed that no remains are interred under the headstone.

What then of the missing PBM-5 Mariner search aircraft? I believe that this was destroyed in a tragic but unrelated accident. Something happened to the Mariner that was so sudden and so catastrophic that there wasn't even time for the pilot to send out a distress message. This was unusual, but it wasn't the first time that this had happened to a PBM-5.

The PBM-5 Mariner aircraft was able to carry up to 3,400 gallons of fuel, giving it immense range but also earning it the nickname *'flying gas tank'* from crews. Fire was a very real risk on the Mariner and several were lost as a result. On July 9th 1945 for example, a Mariner took off from NAS Banana River on a routine patrol mission over the Bahamas. The weather was good but the aircraft was never seen again, no distress message was received and no wreckage was found despite an extensive search operation. An on-board explosion was cited as a possible cause in the subsequent Board of Investigation report. The Aviation Safety Network database lists the loss of 16 Mariners with 126 fatalities between 1943 and 1955, none of which were believed to be due to enemy action.

I think that an explosion on the PBM-5 sent to search for the aircraft of Flight 19 destroyed that aircraft and this seems to be confirmed by the sighting of a burning aircraft crashing into the sea reported by the SS Gaines at 20:00. Just as for Flight 19, rough seas and strong winds would have dispersed any remaining wreckage of the Mariner before a search began the following morning.

.

Conclusion

The disappearance of Flight 19 is a mystery, but not the kind of mystery that involves aliens, UFOs, the Bermuda Triangle or any hint of the paranormal. The real story of Flight 19 centers on the mental state of Lt. Charles Taylor whose continuing, mistaken and nonsensical insistence that Flight 19 were over the Gulf of Mexico led them far out to sea and away from the safety of land. We don't know what was wrong with Charles Taylor that December afternoon, but we do know that something was seriously amiss. He didn't want to fly as the instructor for Flight 19 and when he did, he made a major error by transposing their position in a way that defied logic and reason. The tragedy is directly attributable to this strange aberration.

This wasn't a temporary delusion. From 15:40 on 5th of December, for the short period of his life remaining, the radio transmissions show that Charles Taylor remained absolutely convinced that he knew where he was. In one of the last transmissions picked up from Flight 19 he was heard to say *"I am pretty sure we are over the Gulf of Mexico."* He was completely wrong and it was this mistaken conviction that led directly to the deaths of twenty-seven men.

For the reasons explained earlier, I don't believe that the

wrecked Avengers of Flight 19 will be found somewhere in the Florida everglades. The lack of radio messages after 18:30 almost certainly means they never made it back over land and I think that if they are ever found, it will be on the bottom of the Atlantic Ocean, far to the east of Florida. The increasing sophistication of underwater mapping and survey equipment makes it very possible that someone will one day stumble across one of more of these wrecks on the ocean bed. If that happens, it will finally answer the question of where Flight 19 ended up, but it won't provide the more significant answer of why they ended up there?

It seems probable that the only possible solution to this part of the mystery lies within the field of psychiatry and in the mind of Charles Taylor. There are a number of significant and unanswered questions. Just why didn't he want to fly that day? Did he really receive a letter that morning which upset him? Was his problem nothing more than a massive hangover? What led him to make such a massive error of location between 15:30 and 15:40 and why did he stick to this conclusion so dogmatically in the hours that followed? Unfortunately, without much more information about this very private man, it does not seem plausible that we will ever really understand the reasons for his fatal mental confusion on the afternoon of December 5th 1945. In that sense at least, it seems likely that the disappearance of

Flight 19 will always remain one of the most baffling aviation mysteries.

I hope you enjoyed reading this book. If you did, please take a moment to leave me a review on Amazon. Your opinion matters and positive reviews help me greatly. Thank you.

I welcome feedback from readers. If you have comments on this book or ideas for other books in the Real Story of... series, please send me an email at stevemac357@gmail.com.

Bibliography

Board of Investigation into five missing TBM airplanes and one PBM airplane, convened by Naval Air Advanced Training Command, NAS Jacksonville, Florida, 7 December 1945, and related correspondence. This five hundred page document provides extensive details of the US Navy investigation into the loss of Flight 19 and the PBM-5 rescue aircraft.

The Bermuda Triangle by Charles Berlitz, 1974. Berlitz used Flight 19 as one of the central parts of his contention that the Bermuda Triangle exists and is somehow linked to actions of extraterrestrials. Sadly much of what he wrote about Flight 19 is inaccurate and some of it seems to be entirely invented.

The Disappearance of Flight 19 by Lawrence Kusche, 1980. This should have been the definitive book about Flight 19, but unfortunately, it isn't, quite. Kusche had already written a well-received and sensible book about the Bermuda Triangle (*The Bermuda Triangle Mystery - Solved, 1975*). He was a qualified pilot and in his research about Flight 19 he did what no-one else had attempted – he re-traced the course of Flight 19 over Navigation Problem Number 1 by flying it in a light aircraft. He also spent time with Charles Taylor's family and interviewed other pilots and aircrew with who he had served. However, Kusche seemed to start with the notion that Navigation Problem Number 1 was badly flawed and that it was very easy to get lost. To back-up this notion he made some elementary mistakes. For example, he claimed that *'With the exception of Hen and Chicken Shoals, there were no positive landmarks...'* This simply isn't true. The turning point which began the third leg of the exercise was over Great Stirrup Cay, the route then overflew the island of Grand Bahama and the final turning point was in sight of another large island, Great Sale Cay. The same question was raised during the Board of Investigation and Lt. James Roy Jackson testified that *"With one exception the termination of all legs touch a point of land and that one exception is within sight of a large island."* A good book about this mystery then, but perhaps not a great one.

They Flew into Oblivion: The Disappearance of Flight 19 by Gian J. Quasar, 2005. A sensible, well written and researched book which sets out non-paranormal reasons for the disappearance of Flight 19. Well worth reading, even though I cannot agree with the final conclusion that the aircraft most likely crashed in the Okefenokee Swamp in Florida.

Discovery of Flight 19 (A 30-Year Search for the

Lost Patrol in the Bermuda Triangle) by Jon F.
Myhre, 2012. Another well written, well researched book by
one of the leading Flight 19 investigators. Vietnam veteran
Myhre tells the story of Flight 19 clearly and in great detail,
even if I don't agree with his final contention that he is able
to plot the location of each of the missing aircraft (some on
land in the everglades, some in the ocean).

***The Loss of Flight 19 - Is There a UFO Base Inside
the Bermuda Triangle?*** by Richard Thomas,
publication date unknown. Reading the blurb for this book
probably tells you all you need to know. It notes that an
'entire squadron' of aircraft vanished in 1945 and goes on to
note: *'What is not widely appreciated are the clues that
link the loss to speculation that there might be a
suboceanic base for UFOs in the western Atlantic - right
where the ominous and mysterious Bermuda Triangle is to
be found.'* Avoid.

About the Author

Steve MacGregor is a Scot who writes non-fiction on a range of topics including true crime and mysteries. He has been interested in mysteries since he was around twelve years old and frustrated by the poor quality of most books on this topic since the same time. Steve has worked in the fields of civil and mechanical engineering around the world and his hobbies include restoring elderly motorcycles sports cars, flying and travelling.

He is married with two grown-up children and currently lives in Andalucía in Spain.

Other 'Real Story of...' books

If you enjoyed this book, you may also be interested in these other 'Real Story Of...' books which are also available on Amazon:

The Real story of

The Michigan UFOs

In 1966 events occurred in Michigan that sound like the script for an episode of the X-Files: Over the course of several nights in March 1966 large numbers of people saw strange craft maneuvering in the night skies over remote parts of the state. Several of these witnesses were police officers and at one point a police car chased one of the objects for more than one hour while it was also being tracked on radar by a nearby Air Force base.

Then, US Air Force investigators arrived on the scene and told all the witnesses that they were not only mistaken, they had confused a simple, natural phenomenon with a UFO. Witnesses were angry, bitter and completely unconvinced by the Air Force '*solution.*' It later became clear that the US Air Force had no intention of attempting to identify the UFOs and that they were instead part of a government conspiracy to suppress UFO reports and to ridicule and undermine those who reported them.

High-level recriminations after the event led directly to the closure of the Air Force unit tasked with looking into UFO reports. However, no-one has ever been able to explain just what it was that witnesses saw in the night skies in Michigan in early 1966 nor why the Air Force seemingly continues to use clandestine methods to undermine UFO witnesses and believers.

Made in the USA
Middletown, DE
18 December 2020